Bangs

Amye Archer

Bangs © 2014 Amye Archer. All rights reserved. Big Table Publishing Company retains the right to reprint. Permission to reprint must be obtained by the author, who owns the copyright.

ISBN: 978-0-9904872-7-2

Printed in the United States of America

Cover photo: South Scranton Intermediate School yearbook, 1990
Cover Design: Jennie Barrese

Also by Amye Archer:

No One Ever Looks Up
Shotgun Life

Big Table Publishing Company
Boston, MA
bigtablepublishing.com

REVIEWS

"With frankness, perseverance, and wry good humor, Archer charts her way from betrayal and divorce to new love and motherhood, without ever losing the ability to calculate the losses along with the gains."
~ Christine Gelineau, *Appetite for the Divine*

"There is sorrow and joy and anger in these poems, but always, there is the strength of Archer's voice and her unflinching willingness to cut herself open and bleed beautifully, recklessly onto the page."
~ Roxane Gay, *Bad Feminist*

"Digging down into the turbulent topography of the post-modern family romance, Amye Archer's *A Shotgun Life* is a fiercely honest exploration of the slow motion eruptions and unexpected life events through which we surge as we're carried down the 'darkening road we've yet to meet.' The poems in this volume skillfully portray a burning, fierce loyalty to the lessons (both endearing and enduring) learned from a close study of familial and erotic love – all told through the experienced voice of a narrator whose vision is just clear enough to remind us that keeping the 'ancestral anchor slung over our shoulders' may be the only way to keep us grounded, and in doing so, deliver us safely to our 'new respite from the world.'"
~ Tony Morris, *Back to Cain*

"Amye Archer's *A Shotgun Life* is a fierce little chapbook that will make you climb back, bruised but better because of these poems."
~ *The Collagist*

"Displayed… is a characteristic honesty that can be found throughout the work. This is a fearless self-expression, and it is, for this reader, an abiding quality which sets Amye Archer's *A Shot gun Life* apart."
~ *Pedestal Magazine*

ACKNOWLEDGEMENTS

A writer's heart is never truly their own. Mine belongs to so many people, including:

The community of writers at Wilkes University, especially my cohort: Bill Prystauk, Gale Martin, Ginger Marcinkowski, Ally Bishop, Adrienne Pender, Randy Brzoska, and Rachael Goetzke, who have been the best support system a writer could ask for.

The mentors and faculty at Wilkes University, especially Nancy McKinley, Jim Warner, Sara Pritchard, Tony Morris, Christine Gelineau, Becky Bradway, and Beverly Donofrio, who have guided my writing with patience and encouragement.

My fabulous editor, Robin Stratton, who puts so much passion into every project, and who believed in Bangs from the start. She is a true champion of the arts, and we are lucky to have her voice in our world. My friends and family, especially my partners-in-crime for most of these poems, Jenn Kumpas, and my sister, Jennie Barrese, both of whom have allowed our mistakes, childhood secrets, and teenage indiscretions to be the basis of this book.

Finally, my husband, Tim, and my girls Samantha and Penelope. You have all of me.

This book is for my sister, Jennie, who taught me how to stretch my bangs, get around curfew, and to be an artist.
Thank you for blazing the trail.

TABLE OF CONTENTS

Video Killed the Radio Star	11
Tree Line	12
Eyeliner	14
Heft	16
Maneater	18
Riding in Jeeps with Men	20
Poster Boys	22
With Tongue	24
Pot	25
Mono	26
Bangs	27
Couples Only	28
War	29
Chicken	30
Pockets	31
River	32
Lucky Strikes	34
The Doors Movie, 1991	36
Tesla	37
Watching a Teen Poetry Slam	38
The Fat Girl's Guide to (not) Getting Pregnant	40
Hollow	41
Mad World	42
Salinas Valley	44
A Snow Day Poem	45
Cleaning the Playroom	46
Woe	47
Matchsticks	48
Eating Children on a Fall Day	50
Lost	51
California Dreamin'	52
Milk Teeth	54
Air	55

Video Killed the Radio Star

Tawny Kitaen is sprawled out like a spiderweb
on the hood of David Coverdale's car.
She is wrapped in a cocoon of thin
sheer gauze,
a marshmallow nightgown.
her long legs
pinwheel through the thick night air
like spokes
on a ten-speed bicycle.

I am ten years old
and in my mind,
this is lust,
sex,
love.
I begin to imagine
the same sort of passion
as an antecedent to marriage,
a requirement of matrimony.
I imagine my mother,
angular and square,
like a tower of Legos
crumbling atop my father's 1985 Chrysler K-Car.

Tree Line

When you're on a twilight bus ride from New York City to Pennsylvania, the tree line becomes your timeline. The still-bare branches outside your window rise and fall like seconds.

You remember your fourth grade art teacher, and how she taught you to draw trees by breaking the branches over and over again, fanning the divorces in your family against a construction paper sky.

In sixth grade, you learn to memorize a poem by tapping the beat with your feet.
> *I think that I shall never see*
> *A poem lovely as a tree.*

When you're five, your father plants his feet in the fork of an apple tree, rescuing your cat from the high branches. This singular act will buy him ten years more in your mother's heart.

You meet a boy who hates Robert Frost and loves Kurt Cobain. You marry him.
> *Whose woods these are I think I know.*
> *I've been locked inside your heart-shaped box for weeks.*

You marry the boy who carves your initials in a tree. He teaches you about airplanes. How they can glide onto runways using the tree lines as a guide if all other instruments fail. You memorize the rise and fall of his chest, and measure the rhythm of his breath with your own.

When you're 24, you park your car under a maple tree. The seeds parachute into your engine and you can't leave. You grow into a bad marriage. You choose the path well-traveled. Eighteen months later, you break your own branch.

You remember nothing before the age of four except the bend of your mother's arm and the sound of her voice as she read to you every night.
> *... and she loved a boy very, very much – even more than she loved herself.*

You can paint two things as an adult: the reflection of trees in a lake at dusk, and a rose that looks more like an artichoke.

You're 35 and your daughters plant a pine cone in the soft earth of your yard. Their father swaps the cone with a baby pine in the darkness of night. On the other side of this highway, he waits for you.

When you're on a twilight bus ride from New York to Pennsylvania, and all other instruments fail, the tree line guides you home.

Eyeliner

When Bon Jovi's *Slippery When Wet* album debuts,
it comes with a state-wide mandate to add eyeliner onto your bottom lids.
My sister and her friend of the same name,
corner me in our bathroom with clear, clouded bags of brushes,
pencils, and shades of brown.

I am ten and my eyelids are like peaches.
I blink and bat as the black charcoal tip of a cheap Covergirl pencil
melts along my virgin skin.
like laying down rubber on a road,
the black soot glides to the left
into the crevice of my blink,
the elbow of my wink.
  You have beautiful eyes, one of them says, and it sticks inside of me
like discarded gum.

You have beautiful eyes.

In the mirror I am a supermodel,
the type of girl Jon Bon Jovi might just take home
to his mother.
The girl with the black Vs on her eyes.

Years later, I will be in a bar with sticky jukebox buttons.
   I will play A7, "Livin' on a Prayer," and even though I'm too old to dance in public,
     and I haven't worn eyeliner on my bottom lids since Bon Jovi's *New Jersey,*
I will swirl around like a flower with no stem,
my heels lifting from the cold concrete floor–
Spinning like tops.

A boy with summer hair and winter on his breath will whisper
You have beautiful eyes.
He will push this echo deep inside of me
and I will hold it in my hands like white fuzz
before blowing it out into the thick night.

In the dirty bar bathroom mirror
I am the chunky girl,
the type of girl you send home before the yolk of dawn
cracks completely open.
the type of girl you only find after last call.
You have beautiful eyes, the bartender will say after every other option has left.

My two-year-old twin daughters
are fascinated by my glasses.
They stick their fingers to my lenses
like bugs drawn to a bright light.
They can see themselves
their small faces reflected in my deep brown irises.

"Mommy, pretty," says one.
says the other.
says Jon Bon Jovi.
says the universe.

Heft

There is a boy on top of me
and I can feel
the huff of his breath
the hump of his body
pressing into me
hard and bold
like a brand.

He was not insinuated
not persuaded,
but this is what happens to young girls
with plump little bellies and
small
self-esteems.
We gather up the poison of young boys
With our low cut tops
And desperate eye make-up.

We hold tight against our chests the promise of
popular
pretty,
desired,
wanted.

Be
tween
the ceiling and the floor is my bed
floating like a cloud in the middle of my room while trains and cars
zipper past on the interstate only minutes away
and light years ahead of where I am right now
plunged deep into a pool
of pathetic
so deep
it will be years before I break the surface
clean
to breath the air of self-forgiveness

Because I never said yes
and I never said no–
I simply stayed suspended in that sound
the rush of the traffic
rattling the glass figurines on my dresser

The same way they shake years later
when someone opens and closes the front door
like if they were rushing up the stairs to rescue me
from the weight of the uncertainty
from the memory of my lips silent
from myself
rushing to pluck the pills from my mouth
roll back the clock
and shape my mouth into
a definite
No.

Maneater

In 1984 I place my ear to the floor
as my father's band plays Hall and Oates' "Maneater."
Mona, the singer,
stretches her deep voice like a canvas
over my frame.
In the bedroom behind me,
the trumpet player's wife
holds their new daughter to her naked breast,
the first time I will ever see one.

Oh-oh, here she comes.

The baby is still and the outline of them
vibrates into the light around us.
I roll onto my back, push my head into the soft plush of the carpet
and let my father's snare, and Mona's modulation
move the earth beneath me.

Twenty years from now,
Mona's husband
will be squished like a marshmallow under a fallen car
and her singing voice will swell like a siren
waning between calm and calamity.
My father, divorced, will consider her–
remember the way she sang *Maneater*,
and the music they once made together.

the breastfeeding trumpet player's wife will be an ex wife
and the suckling daughter a juvenile.
a delinquent last I heard.

And one night in my apartment
The oldies station will click to *Maneater*
and I, with the weight of my own divorce on my chest,
will crawl onto my carpet and hear Mona in the fibers.

Riding in Jeeps with Men

I tell my daughters about the bad men
the strangers that will suck them into vans
lure them from my safety nets
rape, imprison, and murder them
carve out their eyeballs with melon ballers–
if they catch even a scent of goodness.
I don't tell them about the cars
the front and backseats I have fumbled over
in my lifetime
The cloth, the leather, the sticky something else of JJ Husker's middle hump.
I forget to mention how my fifteen-year old
thumb,
    wet from my blanket of hairspray
        stuck to the wind like flypaper
        waiting to catch someone sweet.

Or how my friends and I hitched all over town
even though it was the nineties
and dangerous was the adjective fucking everything at the time.

I neglect to tell them how we bummed a ride from a man in a Jeep
with no top
        who looked at us
        ripe in our tight
        jean shorts
and told us he would bring his young daughter along
so we could be sure he wouldn't kill us.
and as we sat topless in that Jeep
windblown down Keyser Avenue,
all I could think about was his little blond daughter
and how her father killing us didn't unnerve her
the way it should have–
and about Amy Henderson's childhood friend
the one they found burned up in a barrel in downtown Scranton
the ghost of the girl

who haunted our parents—
flipped them from sleep to wake
like pancakes
most nights.

We rode in that Jeep for two and a half miles
and when the light popped
to stop—
red
we didn't say thank you or goodbye,
we just tumbled out
 like stones—
our knees scraping the pavement
our palms bloodied.
our lives spared.

I imagine my girls with plump pears
behind their eyes
they stare through me
as if I hold the answer
to why some survive
and some don't.

Poster Boys

My sister and I spend the summer of 1987
wallpapering our shared space
with posters of men in makeup, leather
pants and high hair.
At night, we lie on our soft double mattress,
slide our socked feet along the smooth paper
and swoon over our favorites:
Bret Michaels, Janie Lane,
Axl Rose, Vince Neil, Jon Bon Jovi.

This greatly disturbs my father
who plans on ripping them down
because of the holes
we leave in our bedroom walls
thick with popcorn plaster.

Then, one Sunday afternoon he catches us—
legs planted like tripods on the bed
as we eyeball a particular Motley Crue picture
for signs of too tight leather laces
exposing the slightest sliver of
scrotum.
A promise whispered like tumbleweed
across the cafeteria at school.
Tommy Lee's penis—
if you look hard
enough
stare long
enough
gaze deep
enough—

the flicker of flesh will be there—
under the crisscrossed double X
of skin tight sheepskin.

The next day my father issues
a moratorium
on spandex and leather.
on hairspray and high bangs
on Tommy Lee's scrotum.

With Tongue

I learn to French kiss,
after the school year
has puffed into thin air.
I'm eleven and standing
like a soldier, stiff–
against the plank white siding
of someone else's garage.
Jamie Johnson sticks his thick tongue
like a wet sock
against the inside of my cheek.
 I'm supposed to lick it–
  wrestle with it-
  tie it in knots like a cherry stem.
Hours earlier,
I chose Aerosmith's "Angel"
to represent us–
Named our future children,
Axel and Emily–
matched my first name with his last,
as we truthed or dared our way
to this moment–
and now his clapper rests like a beanbag
against my gums.
And I, having little knowledge
of the intricacies of twisted lips
and pooled spit–
bite when I should suck,
move when I should still,
balk when I should moan.
 "You're doing it wrong," he tells me.
and wipes the blush blood from his mouth.

Pot

My best friend
brings out a white thick
crayon of a joint
stolen from her sister's fringed purse.
"You inhale," she instructs,
"and hold it in."
The smoke swirls in my gut
filling my chest like a hot air balloon
weightless and burning
until the exhale escapes
like helium
through a chorus of coughs and snorts.

In the distance a church picnic—
buzzes like a hive—
bingo, quilts, funnel cakes,
the ticking of a roulette wheel,
Styx begging us to *come sail away*.
Our smoke sits in clouds
like rosary beads
around our necks.
I pinch my fingers together,
close my eyes and suck.
My gummy lips sticking
to white tissue paper thin
zig zag.

Mono

The doctors were unaffected
by the swollen in my neck
the puffed out gills
the golf ball glands.
They stuck a needle in my hand
carrying the juice
that would return me
to well.
For six months—I tip-toed,
around the looming threat
of a larger than life
spleen.
I sashayed my way
through the dim halls
at school
like a ballerina—Pirouetting to protect
the protruding organ.
In the summer
when the swelling subsided
and the spleen
rested safely in its cocoon,
I emerged from my dance—
twenty seven pounds lighter.

Bangs

In 1988,
it's all about the height
the shape
the weight

of the glazed crown
atop my head
bedazzled by dried
drops of crystallized
Aqua Net.

In 1988,
I'm twelve and having the right bangs
is
everything.

My mother hates my hair.
makes me wear a hat—
costing me precious minutes
in the school bathroom-
when I could be smoking,
kissing Paul Duffy,
or stealing candy bars from the corner store.

Couples Only

Skate-away is a buzz
when the purple "Couples Only" sign clicks on
and the beginning chords of
"Honestly" bounce
from girl to boy.
Hot pink wheels
slide to a stop
and perch like pigeons
waiting for the brown wheels
to make their move.

My sister and her boyfriend
glide like cranes
wingtip to wingtip
air between them
around them
under them
as they migrate towards one another.

Her braces blink
pink
green
disco ball blue—
His face shines squeaky with sweat.
Their fingers lock like a knot
as they whirlwind around
swooshing in circles–
flying wingless
over the lacquered floor.

War

1991.

Six of us cram into Lori's Ford Escort.
there are more people than seats
I learn to smoke a Newport
    even though years later I will hear they are made of fiberglass, I will still smoke them.
Lori is my sister's best friend, not mine.
the car is filled with boys I don't know
and suddenly there are warm thighs under the ass of my torn acid-washed jeans.

Over the radio there is an announcement.
We are going to war.
The weight of those words are molasses around us
and the six of us breathe like the air is filled with tar.

2001.

My best friend and I have not spoken in almost six years
but like two clicks of the same gun we are better together–
breast stroking towards one another's unhappy life
like this lake between us is a puddle.

We have lost no one in the attacks.
but the thunder of those towers collapsing make fighting over boys
and bridesmaid dresses
feel like balloons we can bat away with our breath.

Over the radio there is an announcement.
We are going to war.
The hammer slides back and we glide together into the chamber
our fingers intertwined like fused steel.

Chicken

Tragic Tina
tied herself in a knot
on the train tracks—
a hamster wheel
flying backwards
over her teenage lover's head.
dead.
Because
on a saturated Saturday night
in Scranton
train lights
could be cops
stopped
so running
like rats
scattering
scurrying
shoving the beer balls
under our shirts
makes sense.

The news shoots like a cannon down the halls at school
Tina is dead, run over, gone.
She is buried on Railroad Avenue.
An irony lost on us as we stand in pools
of her mother's mascara.
Six years later
my sister still sees her
in nightmares,
our trampled Tina,
wearing a jean jacket
slick lip gloss—
no shoes and
tied to the heating metal
stuck like a stump
dug into the moist earth
of the spring.

Pockets

My sister gets her back pockets ripped off
by an overzealous fan–
at a Tesla concert in Wilkes Barre.
In the sticky August air
she lies on the hood of Ken's 1989 Camero
and cries
she will die
without the black acid-washed
size zero jeans.
The same jeans I work tirelessly
to shoehorn her into
every Friday night
only to have them lie–
minutes later,
on the floor
of Cockroach's van.

River

Bon Jovi's *New Jersey* is the first cassette I ever buy
with money earned
from working the drive thru
at McDonalds.

I listen to "Blood on Blood"
over and over
and then convince Georgia and Dawn to meet me
at the river with stolen razor blades—
where our pink spring blood will drip
into the crisp, cool water
pooling around our bare ankles
mixing, coagulating, before drifting
downstream
like ribbons
to the old Iron Furnaces.

That night, we get high on aerosol,
toss the empty cans in the tall grass
at the same river's edge,
and wade into the gentle waters
with our arms looped
and heads floating like balloons.

Years later,
I will be alone
in a pickup truck
parked crooked in the dirt and
rock
lot
the river still drip-dropping behind me
like a ticking clock-
where my open legs are a moonlit ocean
and boys will fall into me
like waves pounding the shore.

I will sail my mind back
to those three young girls
knee deep in our own
bubbling blood
and I will wonder.
what became of that promise,
those vows to never leave
or run away.

Lucky Strikes

My best friend is Georgia and her dad is dying. He slams his fist over and over again on the cheap wood grain bar where he allows us to drink Schaffer beer and smoke his filter-free Lucky Strikes, even though we are only sixteen and probably close to alcoholics ourselves because what he doesn't know is that we chug down 40's of Crazy Horse in the woods twenty feet from this house almost five nights a week, and that sometimes I puke and Georgia holds my hair back, and sometimes she has sex with someone in the grass off to the left, or maybe it's me, and we fit this all in before curfew. But for him, for my friend's dying dad, we act like sipping a beer is having a boy slip his hand under your shirt for the first time. *HOLY SHIT! This is good stuff.*

The television is what's making him scream and bang his fists, it's hovering over all of us like one of those mirrored convex eye in the sky looking things that dot the ceilings of department stores making sure loose girls don't steal tiny bathing suits they could fit in their wallets. A war movie is on, one with guns and blood and a hot, sweaty jungle swallowing little boys whole like it almost did to him only twenty years earlier, when he was clean shaven and smiling, dressed in a green uniform and heading off to the east coast of Asia. His skin was milk, and the war a nightmare not yet realized.

Now, his fists are sprinkled with Agent Orange and pound with fury against the bar top. Georgia doesn't flinch at words like *Chink* and *Gook*, but I do, they prick at my taste buds like sour milk, like the hard smoke of the Lucky Strike against the back of my throat. My parents don't talk that way. But then again they never held a 105mm Howitzer against the hot throbbing temple of a young woman wearing scraps of a dress with a baby at her breast. They never climbed into a pile of their own steaming shit and burrowed into it like a worm, just to stay alive. But I'm sixteen and buzzed from the Shaffer's, so I let his prejudices slide, and at the end of the night when Georgia's dad reaches the end of whatever road he is revisiting and slips to the floor like an ash falling from the sky, I help Georgia lift him and we carry him like a dead solider to his bed.

Last year, they found him hanging. His fists drained of color, his legs still white like milk.

The Doors Movie, 1991

With Sno-Caps candies pressed like pebbles
into my naked knees
I learn through hushed directives
and a palm on the back of my head
not to bare my teeth.

Break on through to the Other Side.

Tesla

Eugene is Tesla's *Five Man Acoustic Jam*.
His green eyes staring through me on the bus
on the way home from eighth grade is "Cumin' Atcha Live."
Lying hooked in the nook of his arm
on the couch in his basement
smelling of Marlboros and motor oil with
His knees pressed against the back of mine
like the plump part of a comma,
his promises traveling the length of my spine
is "Love Song."

Later, as leaves crash and crush under our shoes,
Missed calls and disappearing acts
become "Signs."
His hand entwined with another–
is right "Before My Eyes."

Watching a Teen Poetry Slam

The teen girls take the stage and they start to rage
about black holes and pits that threaten to suck them down
vacuum them away
like lint.
Backs to walls—
pills to throat, guns to head, razors to wrist,
it is all hard
it is all so hard.
and I sit twenty years from them
but when they read
and the words bleed
from their small mouths like white flowers
planted in poisoned earth
I am two weeks from them
seven days from them
fifteen minutes from them
I am thirty-seven seconds from where they hurt.

I'm fifteen and my skin is as smooth as the sky is wide.
I let a boy define me
drown me
hold me underneath him
under water
under ground
under thick hands and heavy hips
I let a boy
blow apart my world
with the un-zip of his pants.

Now, I see these girls
with eyes like lights
waiting to be dimmed
and I want to save them
to tell them that high school boys will still be
high school boys
at twenty, twenty-five, thirty, thirty-five—
and moments are just that

moments
and this larger than life pain will thin
so keep breathing,
keep breathing.
But I know all I can do is let them balloon with pain
and tie their strings around my wrist so they can never
float
away.

These girls live
in rhymes
These girls live in time
these girls live
where words meet poem
these girls *live*.
These girls *live*.

The Fat Girl's Guide to (Not) Getting Pregnant

Step One: Want it. For years, I imagined Emily following me around with a blanket in her arms like Linus from the Charlie Brown cartoons. Her hair would fall into black ringlets that dripped to her shoulders like water. She would never grow over two feet tall in my mind. She would never get older, never go to Kindergarten, never drive a car, and never kiss a boy. She was a baby, my baby, and I wanted her more than anything.

Step Two: Marry an asshole. Emily's existence was something more than my wanting a baby, it was my need to conjure up a friend, a companion, something to take care of. I was sad and lonely and fat and scared. I was a mess. Emily was supposed to save me from all of that.

Step Three: Have delusions. I had imagined making babies with ease, as if they were simply fruit- ripening on the trees around us–and all I had to do was pluck. I never imagined that skill was involved, that heartbreak was required, and that the one simple accomplishment that came so easily to my mother at seventeen, would be so nearly impossible to me only twenty-some years later. Suddenly there are Basal body temperatures, medication, plotting and charting. It was fucking-tempered with science and biology.

Step Four: Divorce the asshole. The day you left, Emily left with you. The ghost of a child I would never meet. I don't know who I missed more. I cried for you, but I ached for her.

Hollow

As a little girl you dream of babies
filling the space inside of you.
You over-mother your dolls, your little cousin,
a baby bunny you find in the yard.
      (One of these things does not survive your smothering.)
As a teenager, a doctor tells you that your insides
are smooth, black velvet to which nothing will stick.
You let the boys try anyway.
Behind the abandoned fire station,
your skin is a well-traveled galaxy
and "Across the Universe" is your belly.

Nothing's gonna change your world.

You date a boy with little sisters,
swoop them into your arms like fallen stars,
and call them your own.
You brush their hair, long and caramel
with desperate hands that smells like soot.
You cut their crusts, iron their clothes, and hold them against your chest
until they burn away.
As an adult,
you dream of babies–
fill the space inside of you with the wrong men
over
and over again.
Hollow
is the word you burn in sulfur
across the black of the night sky.

Mad World

It's summer now,
    night,
        black and wet.
We have been divorced for weeks,
    months or years,
I've been divorcing you since we met.
We don't talk anymore, yet on this night you are on the burning end of my cell phone. You tell me about a song, "Mad World." It's your song, you say.

The song that describes how you see the world, how you feel it, how it feels you.
It's dystopian, depressed, disillusioned

faces are worn out
and the dreams in which you're dying are the best you've ever had.

Do you still dream that you're dying?
Do you still try to make that happen?
Even though the blonde is pressed against the curve of your back where I used to lie?
Do you remember the day I burst through the door with my lungs on fire?
The pills eating away at your belly? Only *you* woke up.
I walked around with your desire to die like a bubble inside of me, threatening to pop if I sat down too quick or turned the wrong way.

No tomorrow
No tomorrow.

Could it be that easy? Is all of you in that song? Head to wall, wall to head, I banged and banged and banged for you.
Do you have a song? you ask me.
You ask *me*.
You listen for the answer.

Sit and listen.
Sit and listen.

I write my own view of the world,
       I remind you of who I am.
I am the woman who wrote you love poems and pushed them
up into the sky until they fell
like
snowflakes
into ashes.
I'm the woman who held every single piece of you in my hands—
I'm the woman who put pain down like a brand onto paper.
And you forgot that.
Or you never knew it.
Every day I am someone new in the memory of us: a monster, the best lover you've ever had, a cold-hearted bitch, your best friend.
What's my lesson?

Look right through me.
Look right through me.

Salinas Valley

I have a dream that you and I are in California, knee-deep in waves
that push and retract
like lungs.
I think about the time we almost moved there
the salad bowl of the country
a place where things grow and ripen.
I thought I'd plant us there and we'd be okay.
I tell you I love you,
I push it out of me like a baby.
You curl your lips like something bitter is in the air.
I have a dream that we are standing on the rise of something
with waves sucking and blowing beneath us
like we are the King and Queen of our own lives
and the majestic blue is our servant.
I don't dream that you are dying
not yet.

A Snow Day Poem

If there was a way I could take images or memories and implant them
into my daughters' brains without expensive surgery or a lot of pain on
their part,
I would choose the following three moments:

1. The day I first saw them–
   purple and small
   their skin still slick with the insides of me
   my rapid sobs fogging the thick glass between us
   the center of me suddenly collapsing in on itself.

2. The preschool Christmas show.
   They stood apart from me, separate
   out   there.
   and I was in here, all alone.
   The First Noel echoed between us.
   and I swelled with fear
   the way a body holds its water in the wake of a shortage.

3. Now, right this minute.
   When bedtime stories come from their mouths
   and my tongue is silent. When the space between them
   is filled with nicknames for cute boys and stories of lunchtime
   betrayals.
   And suddenly,
   all the pain I have ever felt in my life
   falls away with each whisper I cannot hear.

Cleaning the Playroom

On thousands of sheets of paper you scribble
unicorns with two horns, women with balloon breasts, houses with smiling windows
sticks with jagged hair, triangle skirts, elongated arms with four-finger hands
your name skirts across the bottom like a slick rock on the skin of a lake.
Your five-year-old name.
crooked, ignorant of upper and lower case mingling
free from form.
My heart sinks to the bottom of me
knowing this moment can never still
knowing time will spool away from me
from us
from the two little stick girls clinging to their mommy's four fingers.

Woe

My sick daughter buries her head
under a handmade quilt
while her fever climbs.
and all I can think is that I'm so glad she's not dead.
most nights I dream that aliens snatch her
that she runs into the road two steps longer than my reach
that she screams her throat raw as a fire pulls at her feet
that a van swallows her in the fog of a fall morning
that a hidden vitamin deficiency is creeping through her body
that a teenage boy will say the wrong thing someday and leave her
hanging at the end of a rope
that she will drive recklessly away from something dire.
that she will open her car door into traffic
that she will trip over a Lego and fall down flights and flights
                    and flights of stairs
that she will eat a poisonous mushroom
that she will find her leg stuck in a railroad tie as it heats up
that she will ride her bike off the steep cliff behind our house
and now–
that she will be gunned down learning simple subtraction in her first-grade classroom.
And then, I will have to be that mother
who writes poems and books about her dead child.

Matchsticks

When my kids are gone,
tucked away into the fold of their grandmother's perfectly-pressed sheets,
we have sex.
I'm not talking about "hotel sex,"
because even hotel sex is still tempered with some element of fear.
They can hear us through the walls, or
They can hold us financially responsible for breaking apart their standard queen like it
is made
of matchsticks.
I'm talking about the good sex–
the crazy sex–
sex with no rules and limitless flight
with no tools and no lights
The kind of sex that you never wanted to imagine your parents having.
The kind of sex you have after two bottles of wine and you're too drunk to care about a flabby stomach or what you put in your mouth.
The kind of sex you used to have with people you picked up in bars.
The kind of sex you dream about and never quite wake up from.
The kind of sex–
we used
to have.

When I still wore lipstick for you
and you still shaved for me.
When I could still feel you breathe my name
up and down my spine like dandelions that have gone to seed
and I could feel the thump of our hearts
through our skin so loud and hard that I was secretly afraid they would burst out of us
and sit on my chest like fireworks we would never see again.

Sex like we used to have.
Before you painted my white cabinet red.
Before you changed my tires.
Before you fixed the water heater.
Before you mortgaged me a house.
Before you made me your wife.
Before you made me a mother.
Before you made me.
Before you made me.

Eating Children on a Fall Day

I see the toddlers again this morning
and I can barely control my urge to eat them,
I imagine the flavors of them:

the brunettes tasting like fall
nutmeg, pumpkin spice, the end of something important.
the blondes sweet
like icing smuggled straight out of a can.

I would devour them quickly, stuffing their fighting limbs into my mouth and holding them
deep in my throat until the smell of baby comes floating back up and out like steam.
I imagine the landfill inside of me, large and gaping
and all of the baby parts in the world not filling it up.
I see my girls, growing faster than I will remember it someday-
losing teeth, shedding training wheels, somersaulting sight words off their tongues
leaving baby shaped holes in my gut.
Too big to hold, too big to carry, too big to need me, too big to swallow.

Lost

I am six and the lure of a good candy bar pulls my from my mother's hip and into a story that will follow me forever. How I scream when I turn to find her gone. How I scream even though she is three feet away in the next aisle. How I scream when I think I'm alone. How I scream.

My parents divorce in a pressure cooker. My mother sleeps on the couch, my father searches other women for a trace of her. I am in the garden of their collapsed marriage. It is calm here. My roots stretch out and attach to the wrong man. We survive the blast.

My ex-husband moves out on a Thursday night. I try not to scream when I notice he's gone. I love him in dark, desperate moments. I'll love him forever in 1994.

I am 27 and use my last hundred bucks to buy a black acoustic guitar with a magnet in her hollow belly that pulls boys into my apartment. On a hot fall night one teaches me to play Radiohead's "Creep." He presses my plump fingers down into a flat bar chord and slides our fused hands up and down the thick neck. We make music. I mistake his kindness for love.

I walk the streets with Paul Simon in my ears. Trees hang over me like fallen arches. The sidewalks rip apart from the roots. I worry they will collapse before I make it home.

I am 35 and I write secret letters to my new husband. Letters begging him to hang onto me–like I can anchor us to something concrete. Like I'm not made of tissue paper and gauze, ready to float away in a thick breeze. I fold the notes like footballs and shove them in a forgotten drawer. I save the notes for the other side of this. For the other side of the screams.

California Dreamin'

Dear California,
Every day I have to fight the urge to buy a ticket
and fly into your arms.

Dear California,
I was never a New York City girl,
like I ought to be–
I need space to move around in.
I want to feel your coastline expand inside of my chest.
Let my lungs hammock the rise and fall of your hills
and my breaths clear the smog from your sky.

Dear California,
When I was too young to know what you were–
I wrote about you
like someone had cracked me open and planted you inside
like you were the seedling from which I grew
and I've never stopped reaching for your sunlight.

Dear California,
When NBC's *The Office* chose James Spader to represent you,
I thought to myself: That's *exactly* the right decision.

Dear California,
When the kids came I knew we were over.
that my babes were bulbs planted deeper than I could dig
that if you give a root room to grow
it will devour its surroundings
swallow a mother's silly little daydreams

Dear California,
Every day, every single day,
I have to fight the urge to buy four tickets
and fly us all
into your loving, waiting arms.

Milk Teeth

It's Thursday and your teeth
are gone.
I tuck the last one, the milk tooth I coaxed from your upper gum, into
a Ziploc snack bag
and we slip it under your pillowcase.
You laugh, stick your tongue through the holes in your smile
feel the air brush against the thick tissue.
You've become my great-grandmother–
slippery lips,
and a voice with no bite
sticking me in place with your spit.

Later, I slip my arm under your sleeping head
listen for your measured breaths,
and buy your bag for a buck.

I carry snack bags of teeth in the pockets of my purse–
spread them like ashes.
Bury the baby bits of you in random trash bins
       at the local market–
       your school
       my work
       our neighbor's unsupervised cans

I plant you in the frozen garden
and hope for red, ripe cherries
in the snow.

Air

THICK

At sixteen,
I became a balloon
   sailed in circles over the heads of popular boys who never
      reached
            for my string,

      sunk like a stone in the wake of girls who never
      dragged the lake for proof of life.

My grandfather died that year and after I plucked my sister out of a smoke-filled garage where her teenage boyfriend's band played old Metallica songs with screechy guitars, we mourned and bought dresses. Hers was black and tiny, slid around her hips like a river. Mine was a dark

cave.

THIN

At twenty-six,
the air leaked out and
I became a sailboat
      light and colorful
walking effortlessly on top of the water that once
held me.

A boy with matchstick hair and sulfur breath
lights me on fire and tells me
that I would be beautiful if only I lost twenty-five more pounds.

I want to scream at him and ask him *how much is enough? I have lived on steamed broccoli and water for sixteen months just so I could be deemed attractive enough to be on fire in a bar with a handsome boy. How much is enough? 100 pounds? 200? Should I try to get down to my birth weight?*

I smile and whisper,
Have you read my poetry?
  It will suck your dick for hours
I promise.

THICK

At thirty-six,
I've become a kite
   two bows on my slim string
anchored in the soft palms of my daughters.

I turn myself to the wind
   struggle to float
      up.

The smoldering fire still weighing me down.

ABOUT THE AUTHOR

Amye Archer is a writer and teacher living and working in Northeastern Pennsylvania. She holds an MFA from Wilkes University, and is a recipient of the Beverly Hiscox Scholarship. Her writing has been published in *Nailed Magazine, PANK, PMS: Poem Memoir Story, Hippocampus Magazine, Boston Literary Magazine*, and elsewhere. *Bangs* is her first full-length poetry collection. Amye is the author of two chapbooks, *No One Ever Looks Up* published by Puddinghouse Press, and *A Shotgun Life* published by Big Table Publishing. Her one-act play, *Surviving*, was produced locally in 2012. She has read for various magazines including *PANK, Quiddity*, and *Hippocampus*. Amye is a Libra, a lover of cats, a devout follower of politics, mommy to Samantha and Penelope, and a partner-in-all-things to Tim.

The following poems have been previously published as listed:

NAILED Magazine: "Tree Line", "Milk Teeth", "Heft", and "The Doors Movie, 1991"
Heavy Feather Review: "Riding in Jeeps with Men"
Boston Literary Magazine: "Pot" (Pushcart Prize nominee)
Word Fountain: "Couples Only"
Right Hand Pointing: "Pockets"
The Doctor T.J. Eckleburg Review: "Eating Children on a Fall Day"

www.ingramcontent.com/pod-product-compliance
Lightning Source LLC
LaVergne TN
LVHW091320080426
835510LV00007B/574